ANCHORED IN GRACE:
VERSES OF FAITH AND STRENGTH

Lisa Schermerhorn

BLUEBONNET BOOKS

Dedicated to:

To my girls, Rhonda, Amanda, and Chelsea,
and my husband, Steve.

To God be the Glory

From Lisa's daughter, the Editor and Publisher of this book:

I struggled with this foreword for a good amount of time. Those who know my mother knew various sides of the woman she was— before marriage and kids, before cancer, before Frontotemporal dementia began stealing her away.

She has asked me, because of her dementia and resulting aphasia— the literal loss of her words— to write the foreword and acknowledgements in this book.

I want to honor her, but am struggling to get my feelings in order, as this is the first book I will publish as part of Bluebonnet Books. When I approach my feelings about her life and her work, it feels as though I'm being dragged out to sea by some unseen current. Objectivity is obviously out the window, and it is now up to me to make her life's dream a reality.

For as long as I can remember, she poured herself into words, wanting to publish a book of her photography and poetry. Her poetry is the voice of a mother struggling through severe depression and many other health problems, while dealing with a less-than-ideal marriage, all while trying her utmost to give glory to God.

I have always taken after her, from her physical build to her artistic tendencies in photography and writing— My mother is the reason I am the person I am today. She is by no means perfect, but her love has always been fierce and complete. She took the life she had and came out of it with three fiercely-loving daughters to continue her legacy of loving with Jesus' love.

The fact that I am blessed enough to present her work to you is a testament to God the Father and His unending, unfailing grace and love. With the help of my sisters, I have collected her poetry and various photographs of hers that remain in the following pages. As my mother would want, the refrain of the old hymn, "To God be the Glory," runs through my head as I type this.

In these verses and snapshots of His creation, may God be glorified, and if He sees fit, may her legacy of love live on through us and through her words and art.

Chelsea Schermerhorn
March 2025

Contents

My Love

I noticed you when you first walked in
And you looked around the room
Someone spoke and you turned your head
And your smile lit up the moon
I knew it in an instant,
You were sent for me.
I tried to look into your eyes,
Hoping you would see.
You stepped upon the stage to sing,
The ladies moved in close.
I could never compete with them
I began to lose all hope.
My heart, it sinks,
My lashes catch
The tears that would have been,
I look up just one more time
And melt when you merely grin.
A darting glance and then you pause,
As you look into my eyes,
"You are the one I was looking for?
I never realized.
You are really quite a simple girl,
I never would have guessed,
That you would be the one I sought,
You're nothing like the rest."
My ride is here now,
I must go,
I rise and hesitate.
I see the fear of losing touch
Rush into your face.
I slowly walk across the floor,
Toward the door to leave,
I turn to glance just one time more,
And you're nose to nose with me.
"Hi!"

The Color of Green

Lying in a meadow green,
So deep in grass I can't be seen.
The sun shines high up in the sky,
So bright I can't bear to open my eyes.

Plants around me dance with ease
As prodded by a gentle breeze.
The sound of silence is all around.
I fall asleep upon the ground

The warmth of the sun,
I wiggle my nose.
A butterfly flutters
Around my bare toes.

A smile on my face awakens me
As on-looking wildlife
Scurries to bushes and trees.
The air I breathe in is crisp and pristine.
This, to me, is the color green.

What Dreams Are Made Of

Magic carpets, time machines,
Touching stars and moon so high,
Lying in meadows and singing songs,
Or just moving your arms to fly,

Painting pictures with the clouds,
Observing the change of seasons,
Bursts of laughter, right out loud,
For no apparent reason,

Closing your eyes and knowing,
There is nowhere you cannot go,
Spending winter in the mountains,
Building snowmen in the snow,

Sitting in a garden,
And smelling the fragrance there,
Hearing the sounds of nature,
Feeling love is in the air,

Hypnotizing flames that dance
Upon an open fire,
Writing music or poetry
At the moment you feel inspired.

Having a friend to understand you,
No matter what you say or do,
Hearing them as they whisper,
"No matter what, I love you too."

This is what "DREAMS ARE MADE OF"

The Song

Listen to the music.
Hear the words.
They ring so true.
Feel your heart throb, with the beat
Of the drum
And know THE SONG was written for you.

Its not another cheatin' song
Or of righteous indignation.
It's a song of unconditional love
That is straight from your imagination.

Listen to the music.
Hear the words.
They ring so true.
Feel your heart throb, with the beat
Of the drum
And know THE SONG was written for you.

How did they know,
Where to put that pause,
And just the right words to sing?
Seems as if they opened your heart
For everyone to see.

Listen to the music.
Hear the words.
They ring so true.
Feel your heart throb, with the beat
Of the drum
And know THE SONG was written for you.

LIFE IS GOOD!

Life is good.
I woke up.
I am still functioning.
I do not know where my next step will take me
Or if I will take a next step.
I will endeavor to
Make the most of life.
And to be clear in my thinking
And to move towards my goals today
For tomorrow may never come for me.
I will be sober and vigilant
In respect for my family and loved ones,
That I can make the time I spend with them
A time of quality memories
And make the things I achieve in my life
The best they can possibly be.
I will appreciate the beauty around me
And not take any of God's creation for granted.
I will not quench any emotion.
Happiness, love, sadness, loss, anger;
I will embrace them all,
For all of them reflect life and passion.
Life is Good!

Storm

The rain has halted,
The wind has eased,
All that remains is a cool, gentle breeze.

The thunder subsided,
The lightning ceased,
All there is now is a cool, gentle breeze.

The trees have quit dancing,
And the flowers are at peace,
All there is now is a cool, gentle breeze.

The dust is all settled,
The air is so clean,
All there is now is a cool, gentle breeze.

God has been here
And has left His spirit,
The cool, gentle breeze.

These Dreams Will Last

Fix me up a wooden shack,
Put horses in the field,
Wildflowers for decorations,
Underneath the window sill.

Fill the skies with fluffy clouds.
Let the rays of the sun peek through,
The warmth of them upon my face; I think
A song would be nice too.

A bench in the midst of a garden
A moon and the stars at night
Sitting there in silence
Life seems so perfect and right

Acting on an impulse,
Knowing these dreams, as memories, will last,
We look into each other's eyes

And wash our faces in the dew of the grass.

The Summit

I see the top!
I can do it!
It's just a mountain I have decided to climb.
I won't rest now, 'til on the summit I lay,
becoming one with the rock, as in my mind.

The odds are against me
Before I start,
I am weak, my load heavy, with pain.
I look to the mountain;
Again see the top,
I have nothing to lose; all to gain

Don't push me. Don't pull me
I'll go my own pace.
It's to accomplish a goal, for me,
Not a race.

Don't tell me I can't,
For I will, you will see.
Nothing but death
Can hinder me
All things accomplished
Must first have been dreamed.

Higher

I climbed upon a rock today
To look across the sea
Not knowing what I thought I'd find
Nor what I wished to be.
The climb was steep in places
The rocks, like knives were sharp.
Determined to see across the sea
I climbed with all my heart.
My goal intense, my legs grew weak,
Some places I had to crawl.
I would not give in, my mind made up
I had to give my all.
Once on the top,
I looked around to see if I could see
Just exactly what it was
That diligently prodded me.
Where you were, I could not see,
But the voice I heard so clear
"Dare to dream, believe, set your mark higher"
Was whispered in my ear.

Security

Gentle rain upon my face,
Brings peace and knowledge
Of God's grace.

Rolling thunder is peaceful too
The voice of God
Rings clear and true.

A streak of lightning
Across the sky,
God's in control,
From His throne on high.

In this, I find security.

PEACE

Sheer frustration, agony and pain
Just when you think the sun will shine
Here comes the rain

I sit and think, "what do I do?"
And then I think some more.
And all at once, going on my knees
I drop and hit the floor.

I look up, and there You are,
In control and so very strong,
It makes me wonder why coming to You
Has taken me so long.

But I am here now, and feel the peace
That Your presence brings
It is like the voice of a babbling brook or
Birds that sing in spring.

I see You reach, and I reach too,
And You gently touch my hand
And then it is that I receive the truth
That You brought to man.

"I AM."

THE STORY OF THE STONE WALLS

The air is damp and musty here,
I taste mildew in the air,
I touch the walls of stone,
And feel the story there.

I feel the love that built the walls
The pride, the motivation,
I see the glow upon his face
And the builder's dedication.

He built a home, not just a house
A place of peace that was safe,
A place for love and family,
That would withstand centuries of war and waste.

The battles they have been through,
Only the walls can tell,
The story is there if you take time
To listen and taste and smell.

I cannot tell the story,
I couldn't even start,
The story here is hidden
And heard only with a heart.

The Battle

The trumpet sounds,
The battle begins
Thunder of horses' hooves
Vibrate the land.

Over and through mountains
Arrows unceasingly fly.
A rock is thrown,
It blackens the eye.

Vision is blurred and
The pain is intense.
The spirit is wounded,
Defeat is imminent.

The wound is much worse now,
Than thought from the start,
The cut to the eye
Has severed the heart.

The warrior collapses,
Exhausted and spent.
She sleeps for a while,
An angel is sent.

Healing will take time,
But the battle is done.
The enemy's defeated
By the Sword, God's own son.

Rise and Stand

A single tear rolls down her cheek,
She's trying to be strong.
You pull her up against you
And promise to not be long.

Somewhere deep inside, she knows,
That time will come to a stop.
You realize her fears as your arms
From around her drop.

She shivers, and then she wipes the tear,
And smiles a crooked smile,
Shuddering, she turns her back,
Pretending happiness all the while.

Once you're out of sight it seems,
Her strength just falls away.
She falls upon her knees,
And this is what she prays.

Tell him that I love him, Lord,
Each moment of the day.
Remind him that I wait for him,
When temptation comes his way.
Make him true and faithful, Lord;
I put him in Your hands.
Because You do this for me, Lord,
I have strength to rise and stand.

Quiet Place

There's a quiet place in my spirit,
I struggle to attain.
Situations seem to come and go
I'm certain, tomorrow will change.

Where is the balance in all of this?
Where do I go for rest?
When will it all be over?
Will I be able to pass the test?

I see the storm approaching.
My bones, aching with the thought
Of the turmoil traveling in it
And the battle that must be fought.

Ephesians 6: 13-18
13 Wherefore take unto you the whole armour of God, that ye may be able to withstand in the evil day, and having done all, to stand.
14 Stand therefore, having your loins girt about with truth, and having on the breastplate of righteousness;
15 And your feet shod with the preparation of the gospel of peace;
16 Above all, taking the shield of faith, wherewith ye shall be able to quench all the fiery darts of the wicked.
17 And take the helmet of salvation, and the sword of the Spirit, which is the word of God:
18 Praying always with all prayer and supplication in the Spirit, and watching thereunto with all perseverance and supplication for all saints;

The "Quiet Place" is within me,
It's a place I choose to be
When I obey the word of the ALMIGHTY GOD
And let IT set me free.

One Tear

There's but one tear left in these eyes to cry
One tear they both must share
Just one droplet of moisture,
It's all this heart can spare.

One tear now has a purpose
Other than to release my pain.
For in it life is reflected
And its hope now makes me sane.

So, if one tear is all you have left,
Don't waste it, let others see,
And let it mirror your strength and your love
As you choose to live and to be.

Square Peg

A square peg does not fit into a round hole.
If it is put into one in which it will slide into,
There will be empty spaces surrounding it and
It is easily seen by all that it is an unnatural and inadequate fit.
If it is forced into one (hammered) it may fill up all the space,
But the edges of it will be permanently damaged
And it loses its identity as a square peg.

Sovereignty

Why do my eyes go on crying
When all I want to do is smile?
Why is my heart feeling heavy?
Maybe it will pass in awhile.

I try to keep my mind busy,
While the weight of the world presses in.
The joy that I seek eludes me it seems,
The present is tearful and grim.

What do I need to get back on track?
What can I learn where I am?
Is there something I am missing that I need to know?
Ha! I hear You "I AM."

I'll travel this road a while longer,
As I struggle for independence supreme.
Contentment is a decision I must make for myself
As I struggle for sovereignty.

sov*er*eign*ty n, pl -ties 1 : supremacy in rule or power 2 : power to
govern without external control 3 : the supreme political power in a state

Sinking

Slowly, I descend.
My feet disappear.
My legs try to move,
Why they won't is not very clear.

My knees get stiff
And will not bend.
My hips are covered now.
It all will soon end.

I look around for help,
As my chest is almost gone.
My heart is still beating,
But I am all alone.

The earth is swallowing me up.
I am sinking.
Deeper and deeper I go.
My hands covered, now
I cannot feel.
Soon I will cease to breathe and think.
Someone dig me out, please.

Crying on the Inside

I am crying on the inside,
Filling my heart to the top with tears,
I can hear the sound as falling rain drops
Pounding in my ears.

My heart, it beats so hard and long,
So burdened with the load,
It begins to drip the tears.
And they travel to my toes.

My body fills up quickly.
Just an empty cavity.
As my heart beats a little faster,
The tears rise to my knees.

Now the tears, they spew right out
And the salt is starting to sting.
It seems as if I'm paralyzed.
I can hardly see a thing.

The tears are overflowing now,
And I thing that I shall drown,
For as the tears get deeper,
I sink into the ground.

The Living Dead

Rip out my heart
And tear it to shreds,
And give it to me with a frown.
Put me off, then bury me
Six feet underground.
Shovel it in and cover me up,
I'm used to it, so it's okay;
How many times must I die
Before I go away?

Start Again!

So tired of fighting
This feeling I have inside
To just give up and quit
And leave it all behind.

Just breathing overwhelms me
And dreams are so far away.
It seems the more I reach
The further they move away.

A spectator of my own life,
How did this get to be?
I look down and there I am
At a crawl on my hands and knees.

"It's a cold, cold comfort"
"Can't always get what you want"
"But I'm not giving up and you're not giving in"
You lift me to my feet and say,
"It's time to start again!"

Forgive Me

So many times in my endeavors,
My flesh gets in the way.
So many opportunities
Have been lost from day to day

I ask you now to forgive me Lord,
For the ones I've led astray.
Send someone to guide them Lord
Back to You today.

Make my love a perfect love,
I yearn to be like You,
It's a burning in my spirit, Lord
To be tested, tried, and true.

Amen.

EMPTY

When there's nothing left but your empty shell
Where your person used to be
That is when I come to you
And fill your every need.

When you have no more strength to draw from
When you're less than weak, you're dead
That is when I do my works
In your heart and not your head.

There's nothing your thought can accomplish
There's no way up but Me,
And it's when you become an empty vessel,
And fall from bended knee.

You'll feel My arms around you
And my new wine pouring in.
I'll make you what you're supposed to be,
And free you from your sin.

So lift your eyes to Mine, my child
I've readied the best wine to pour,
Drink of Me til overflowing,
Thirst again no more.

The Sound of Cold

The creak of a tree branch
Burdened with snow,
A gasp.
A shiver,
The sound of cold.

Blue

I am sometimes a mood you cannot shake
Yet I am the paint on a beautiful lake
I am recognized in a fresh new bruise,
I'm a song that is sung which is sad, but true.
I am found in the rainbow,
And the sky is my hue.
I call you to flight.
I am blue.

WEB

Kick and crawl and spin and toil
For invisible art and walls that are spoiled.
Catch and wrap things
Tight and secure,
Feed, breed, and die.

IT'S ONLY A DREAM

I think of you in the morning
Before I open my eyes.
I try to imagine me wrapped in your arms,
And then I realize;

It's only a dream.
It may never be,
But I long for it every day
I can't get you out of my thoughts for a moment.
I wonder if you feel the same

I think of you in the afternoon
As I sit down to rest and to eat.
I try to imagine you next to me
I look over to an empty seat.

It's only a dream.
It may never be,
But I long for it every day.
I can't get you out of my thoughts for a moment.
I wonder if you feel the same.

I think of you as the day nears its end.
I want to tell you I care.
I turn to talk to you.
Why am I surprised
When you are not really there?

It's only a dream.
It may never be,
But I long for it every day.
I can't get you out of my thoughts for a moment.
I wonder if you feel the same.

She Runs Away

A bump, a thud, a small cry, a moan,
It's happened again,
The King has left His throne
To reign justice upon His subject?
Only His eyes see the wrong,
His own humiliation,
For she refuses to be controlled.
For His subject,
A choice is made on this dark and dreary day.
She runs away.

Strangers

A bump at my door,
I say, "Come on in.
It's been a while…
Yes, where all have you been?
Just drop your bags right there on the floor.
Let's sit right here, while you tell me more."

I take a deep breath, and give a little sigh
Oh baby, I've missed you, is what's really on my mind.
But I just hold back to see what you say.
It seems like we're strangers,
It shouldn't be this way.

You tell me how, you've been here and there,
But for some reason, Darlin', my heart does not hear.
My eyes mist up as they look on your face.
If I could just touch you,
Things would fall into place.

Then you stand up, and grab me by the arm,
You look me in the eyes and say,
"I don't mean you any harm,
But Baby it's been a long time for me
And I want you so bad that
I can hardly see.

Every time I closed my eyes,
I imagined you,
Right there beside me Darlin',
That's how I got through.

I'm not gonna wait any longer,
I'm takin' you right here,
You're my one and only Love,
I want to make that clear."

You take me in your arms then,
And I begin to cry.

The tears that once just misted,
Fall freely from my eyes.

I was afraid you would not remember
The way it was before.
I thought you might forget met
The minute you walked out the door.
But Baby, I was hopin', you still feel the way I do.
And then you looked into my eyes and that… is when I knew.

We are not strangers,
Not lovers in the night,
You are my husband and
I am your wife.

Truth

I whisper in your ear.
I smile when you are near,
I reach out to bring you in,
When you wander too far from Me.
I let you go just far enough,
To bring you to your knees.
I lift you and embrace you,
And hold you close again.
I love you, My child.

REALITY

I take a flying carpet and
Fly up in the sky
I just can't get where I want to go
I just can't fly that high

So I take off for the mountains
And hike through the forest quick
Until I see a clearing
Where the grass is nice and thick

The flowers that surround me
Sway and dance to the rhythm of the breeze
I lie upon the ground here
And look into the trees

I have been so lonely,
Though people are all around
I could not be comforted til
I laid upon this ground

It is here I have the company
Of one who understands
For nature itself seems to be
My one and only friend

I have been accepted here
For who and what I am
One day I will return to it
And become part of this ground

I have decided to never finish this poem. There is too much pain involved.
I have awakened in the middle of a dream and am back in reality now. Love
hurts and people will always fall short of being a fulfillment to your needs. I,
now back in reality, will endure the pain and I will survive the hurting that
goes along with loving.

Some day I will become part of the earth again, and then, there will be no
more pain.

BLESSINGS SENT HER WAY

She gets up in the morning
And everything's okay.
She stops to sit and think awhile
And her smile begins to fade.

What you think is on her mind
Is there…it's not denied.
She shakes herself to get a grip
And continues on awhile.

She struggles with the pain of the past,
What can the future hold?
She kisses all her loved ones goodbye
And tells them she loves them so.

She goes outside to get the mail
Later on that day.
Then she sees some butterflies
Who seem to be at play.

She thinks they are so peaceful
But has come to realize,
They are struggling the same as she
Just working to survive.

So she makes it one more day,
Stars and dreams a grasp away.
She says a prayer and thanks the Lord
For the blessings sent her way.

How Low Can I Go?

How low can I go?
There is no bottom it seems.
Is there no end to the falling?
I can't even remember my dreams.

My "I wish" is empty.
There is no "I want" anymore.
Just falling with nothing around me;
No ceiling, no walls, no floor.

How low can I go?

ME

How do you reclaim passion,
When it's fallen by the way?
How do you get the courage
To start a brand new day?

How do you start to feel again
When you're numb from pain of past?
How do you let go of who you were
When you seem to have changed so fast?

As I stand before my mirror,
There's a face I notice there.
I don't recognize the features
Or the empty, icy glare.

Will I ever be familiar
With the person I've come to be?
Will I ever find pieces of the kid I was
In the person I now call ME?

ME, YOU NOT LOVING ME

Hanging from a ledge,
Falling endlessly,
Buried alive,
Swallowed by the sea.
Me, you not loving me.

I am a Rose

I am a red, red rose
Opening a little every day
And just when I open fully,
My petals will fall away.
Will I cease to exist?

Pain

The pain is sharp and constant.
It will not go away.
I tell my heart to stop it now,
Hurting is not the way.
My shortened breath is wasted,
My heart continues on,
Pumping tears up to my eyes.
I feel so all alone.
The rhythm has increased its pace,
Spilling tears upon my face.
I thought I had but one tear left,
I guess I was mistaken,
It seems that tears are infinite
When someone's heart is breakin'.

Escape

Take me away, please take me now
Before I lose my way.
Show me the place I need to be
To start a brand new day.

A place where smiles are plentiful,
And free to pick up and wear,
A place where all burdens are light
Because someone always shares.

Take me, just refresh me, please;
Just a little hope, and a bit more time.
A simple life is what I seek
Slower, with some peace of mind.

Even in my summons to You,
My plea is full of haste.
I, anxiously, await Your arrival to
Take me to this escape.

SEARING BRAND

I have a searing brand
Embedded in my heart.
I tried to cut it out,
But it's forever of me a part.

LOVE IS A CONDITION

Love is a condition
It's as fatal as can be
A disease that takes over your being
Once you are infected, there is no getting free.

You can struggle and fight against it,
You can say it's just not so
But truth is, if it gets you,
It'll never let you go.

So if you see it close to you
Don't catch it, try to flee,
'Cause if it gets a grip on you,
You could just cease to be.

LOVE IS ALWAYS GAIN

Love is an open heart
Left wide with plenty of room
For the object of love to sever and slash
The flesh therein.

Love is putting it all on the line
Risking all you are to trust,
And to smile, just one more time.

Love is still caring when the flesh is torn
And mangled from lies and deceit;
And the ache in your heart makes you vulnerable and weak.

Love is never a waste or a loss,
No matter what the cost or pain.
Love, unconditional love, is always gain.

Whisper

In poems I've written in the past,
I spoke of tears and life and dreams.
I even spoke of mountain tops,
Of tough times and times my heart screams.

It's been awhile since I've expressed
The emotions held deep within.
Ever present, though they are,
Entwined and tangled to no end.

Be loosed, I speak now,
Emotions of my heart.
Oh Spirit of God release them.
Bind all confusion and fear
And send again Your message to me
Whispered in my ear.

Amen.

Legacy

I leave you with a piece of me
That time can never fade.
I leave you with my heart
That never can you trade.

I empty out my thoughts
And those I leave you, too.
And the words spilling from my mouth
Spring forth from life and truth
But never shall you fathom the depth of my
"I love you!"

Lisa Finkenbinder Schermerhorn is a woman of unwavering faith who has devoted her life to God. She is married to Steven Schermerhorn, and together they have three children: Rhonda Mills, Amanda Fitte, and Chelsea Schermerhorn. Lisa is also a proud grandmother to three grandchildren—Aaron Mills, Liam Hall, and Kavik Fitte.

A graduate of McGregor High School in McGregor, Texas, Lisa later pursued photography courses at McLennan Community College. She has always had a deep passion for both poetry and photography.

Lisa's journey has been marked by resilience and faith. She was first diagnosed with breast cancer in 2005 and later faced breast cancer again, followed by kidney cancer. In 2017, she was diagnosed with Frontotemporal Dementia (FTD). Through every challenge, Lisa has remained steadfast in her trust in God, drawing strength from her faith.

This book marks Lisa's debut as a published author, though her poetry has already touched many lives. Her poem Blessings Sent Her Way was transformed into a song by musician Harry Booth, a testament to the power and beauty of her words.